Virtual Conference

Class & Course Notes:

Journaling & Planning Notebook

Journaling Scribbles Collection

scribble your name:

Address:

Dates:

An artist and writer's

copyright

encourages a culture of support

and honors the person

who creates, writes, & designs

publications & works of art.

Cover design, artwork, and interior formatting by Patricia Tiffany Morris, owner of Tiffany Inks Studio LLC.

Tiffany Inks Studio LLC
PO Box 299
Bondurant, IA 50035

ISBN: 978-1-955274-21-0

www.patriciatiffanymorris.com

Endorsements:

"**An inspiration station** for contemplators, doodlers, journalers, planners, dreamers, and creatives of many kinds who want to renew thoughts and cultivate gratitude in a hands-on way. Patricia inspires and guides with a variety of ways to combine art, bible study, prayer, contemplation, dreaming, and goal setting all based on Philippians 4:8.

I particularly love that she's provided a little help for those who are just getting started with adding lettering and drawing in their spiritual practice."

~**Ginger Harrington :** Author of **Holy in the Moment** (GingerHarrington.com)

"**With breathtaking beauty,** Patricia Tiffany Morris has created page after page of prompts that invite you to open your mind and pour out, gather, and organize thoughts, plans, feelings, and details of your life. The stunning pages in Journaling Scribbles elevate my mind-musings to a whole new level that compliments the busy neurology going on, even in my dreams.

Studies show the act of writing, gripping a utensil, and tapping into our inner world, spilling out our thoughts, activates parts of our brain that reduce stress, increases wellbeing, organizes the chaos of uncertainty, and increases our ability to reach our goals.

What an incredibly beautiful way Patricia Tiffany Morris has created to help us "mind-map" what we think... and show us who we are. My thoughts never looked so good! What a wonderful thing to pick these books up in years to come and say, "Yes, that was me!"

~**Deborah McCormick Maxey, PhD:** Licensed Professional Counselor, Licensed Marriage and Family Therapist , and Author of **The Endling** (DeborahMaxey.com/books)

"**If you are looking for something to jumpstart your journaling process,** Patricia Tiffany Morris has the answer in this series of journals. Beautifully illustrated with Patricia's own art, you're sure to discover a creative way to organize and process your busy days in a way that fits your lifestyle."

~**Mary Potter Kenyon :** Program Coordinator for Shalom Spirituality Center, certified grief counselor, Therapeutic Art Coach, and author of seven books, including **Called to Be Creative:** A Guide to Reigniting Your Creativity (MaryPotterKenyon.com)

"**As you open this book you realize; each page is an invitation to dance.** Patricia Tiffany Morris is a wonder. Since the moment we met, I've been constantly astounded by her capacity to pour out her zeal to encourage and build others up. Some might be content to create whimsical and inspiring art, and stunningly beautiful poetry and prose, then sit back and enjoy the accolades and awards that go along with it.

Not Patricia. Sure, she's got those too. But she's busily passing out keys to the Kingdom in every way she can, that our own art, writing, and our relationship with Jesus, might flourish. Social media trainings. Tech trainings. Biblical devotionals. Now, her creativity and planning journals, diaries, & sketchbooks.

I strongly recommend you snap up an armful for all the dreamers and the doers in your life. And for all you artists, here's the really unique thing about these journals: Patricia knows how the creative mind works and celebrates it! Well done, Patricia."

~**Wendy Hibbard :** Founder, The Writing Room and SHP Coaching; Editor, **Beneath the Mask:** Faith, Hope & Transformation in the Face of COVID-19 (wendyhibbard.com)

to the One who created all things and for His glory.

journaling scribbles™

A Collection of Notebooks, Journals, Logbooks, & Planners for Creativity & Organization

Patricia Tiffany Morris

Published by Tiffany Inks Studio LLC ©2021

gratitude

Filling the spaces between us.

Special appreciation to my endearing husband who offered his humor, puns, encouragement, and keen poetic insights from conception to publication.

To Terha Knittel, lovely composer and vocalist extraordinaire, who composed the music in the video promotions and for my book trailers, and her son, Kyle who guided me through many hours of video production.

To Rachael Colby who spent long hours reminding me that I can't give up.

To Elaine Giles for her tutorials on YouTube and teaching others about Affinity software, Scrivener, and sharing many other tech tricks.

To KG Fonts, FontSpring, and others for the stress free licenses.

To my launch team and FB group who helped proofread, edit, and cheer me toward and through publication. My gratitude to these idea generators, amazing brainstorming networkers, and the many cheerleaders, formatting ninjas, and "let-it-be-enough" believers, trust soldiers, and prayer warriors. You are treasured and loved. Thank you from my heart and soul.

to the One who created all things and for His glory.

Color, scribble, sketch, draw, & write ideas on the following pages.

Table of Contents

Notebook at a Glance

Table of Contents
Notes Section and Overflow Notes
GO-TO Section Block at Bottom of Page.
Doodling & Coloring Center Section.
Reference Section of Ideas and Inspiration.
Planning & Goal Setting.
Next Steps Action Planning

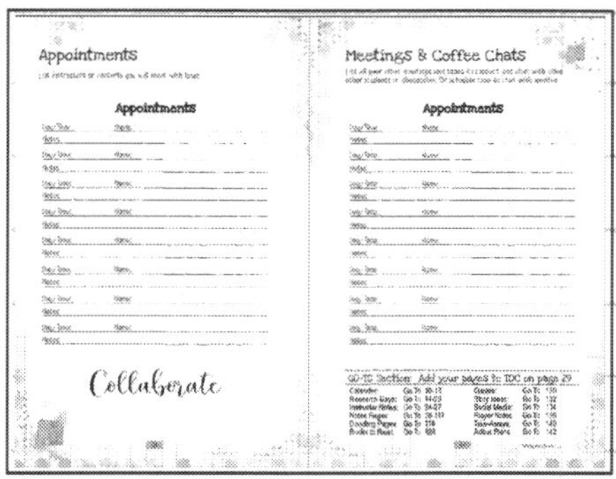

Appointments & Planner Pages

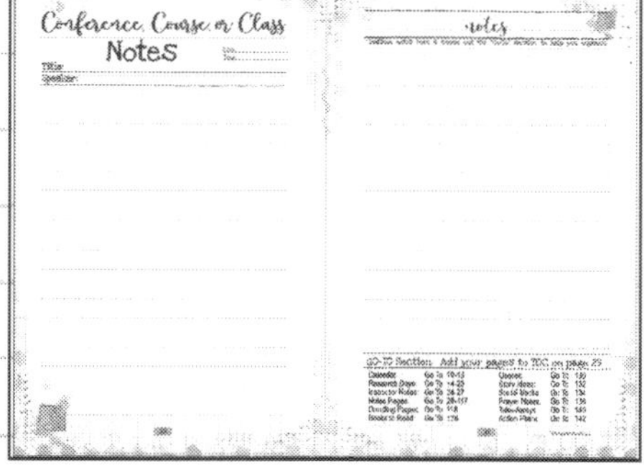

Notes & Go-To Feature

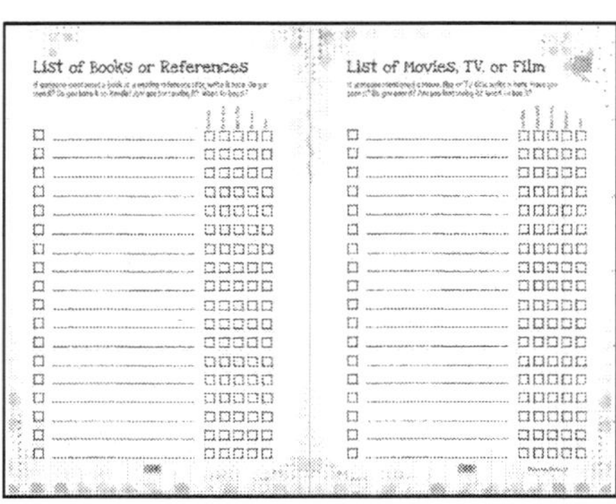

Books to Read & Resources

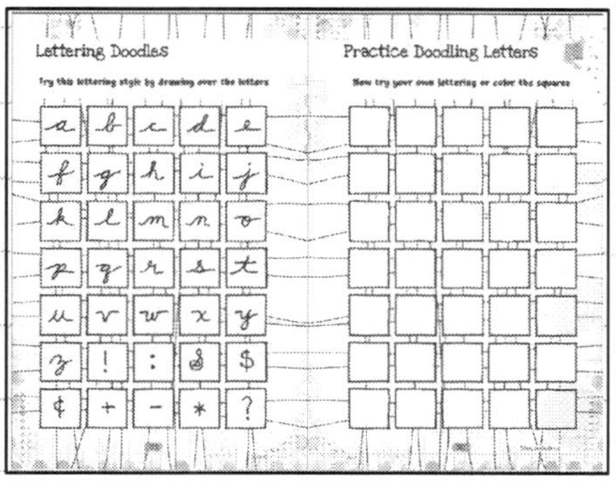

Doodling Pages

Class or Course Information

Use this page for listing course platforms and URLs.

websites

- [ ] Udemy: https://www.udemy.com
- [ ] Skillshare: https://www.skillshare.com/
- [ ] Coursera: https://www.coursera.org/
- [ ]
- [ ]
- [ ]
- [ ]
- [ ]
- [ ]
- [ ]
- [ ]
- [ ]
- [ ]
- [ ]

Wish List for Online Studies

List activities to try and skills you'd like to develop.

possibilities

- [ ]
- [ ]
- [ ]
- [ ]
- [ ]
- [ ]
- [ ]
- [ ]
- [ ]
- [ ]
- [ ]
- [ ]
- [ ]
- [ ]

Calendar for the Year:

Fill in the name of the month & the days for the year you will track.

Month:

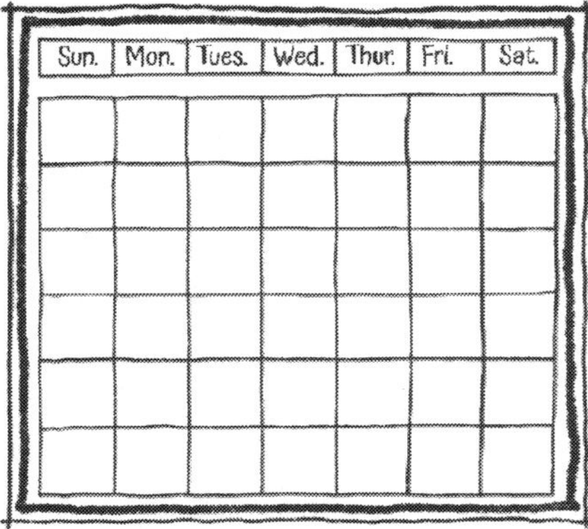

Month:

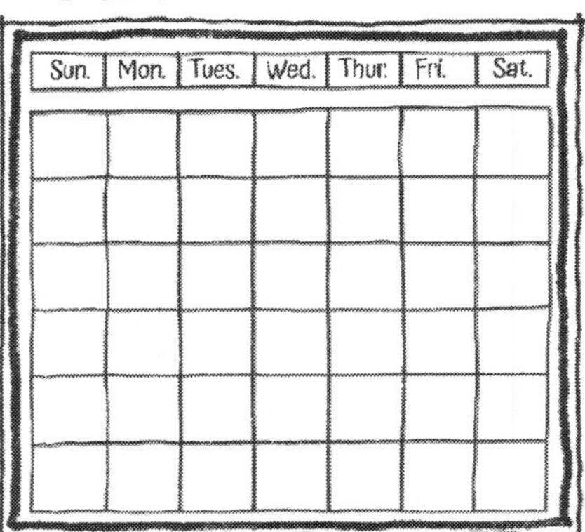

Month:

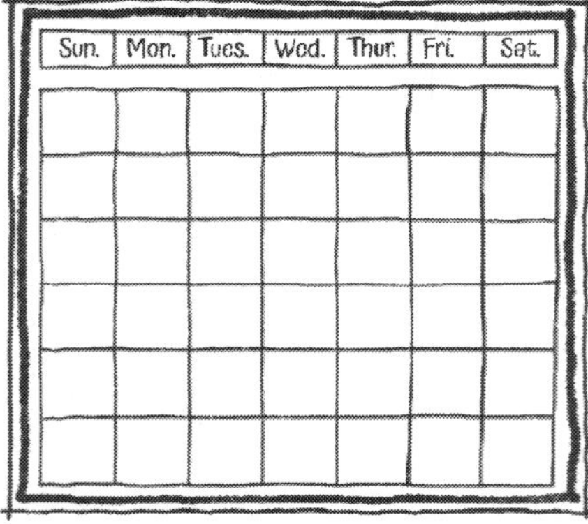

Month:

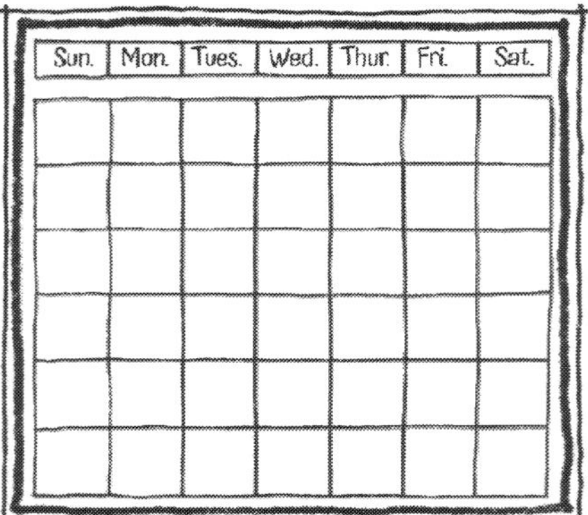

Month:

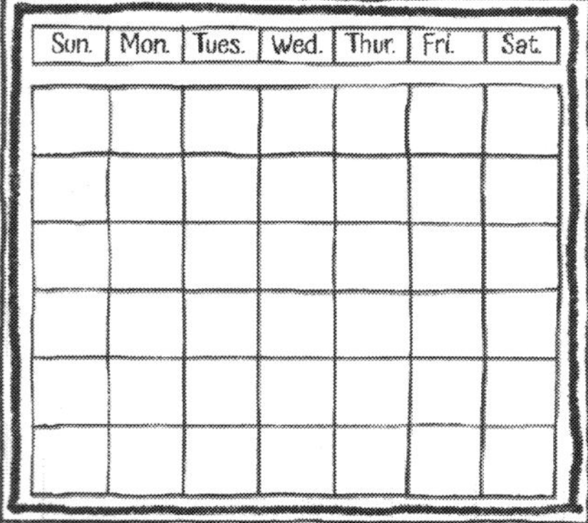

Month:

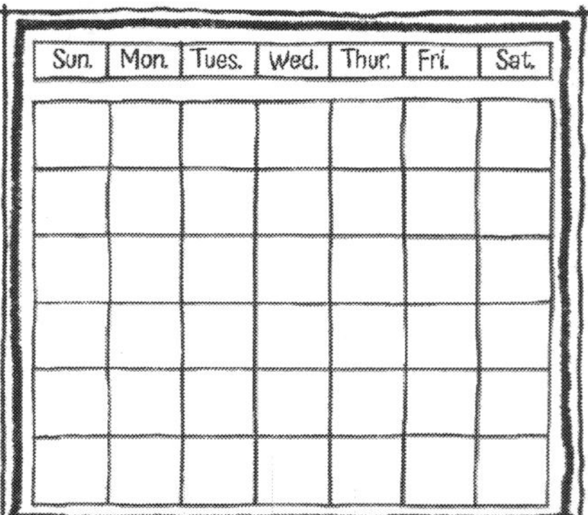

Events & Important Dates

Record events & important deadlines for the months you will track.

- [ ]
- [ ]
- [ ]
- [ ]
- [ ]
- [ ]
- [ ]
- [ ]
- [ ]
- [ ]
- [ ]
- [ ]
- [ ]
- [ ]
- [ ]
- [ ]

Calendar for the Year:

Fill in the name of the month & the days for the year you will track.

Month:

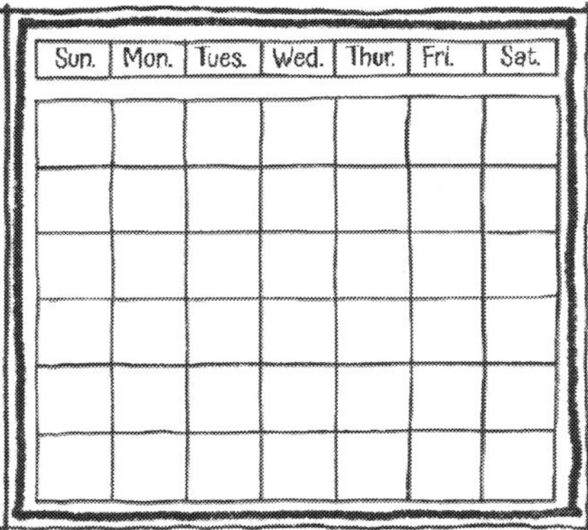

Month:

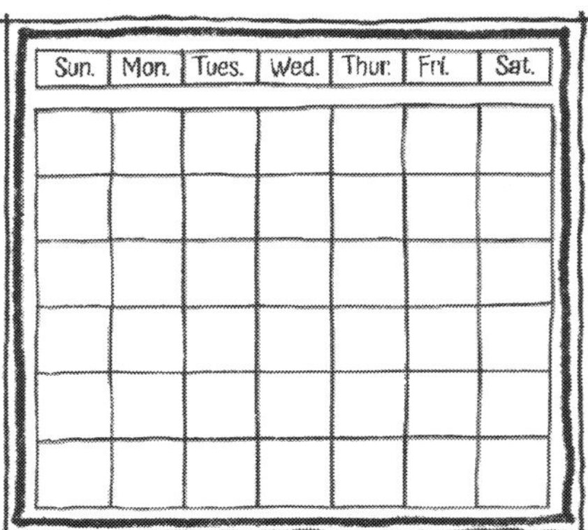

Month:

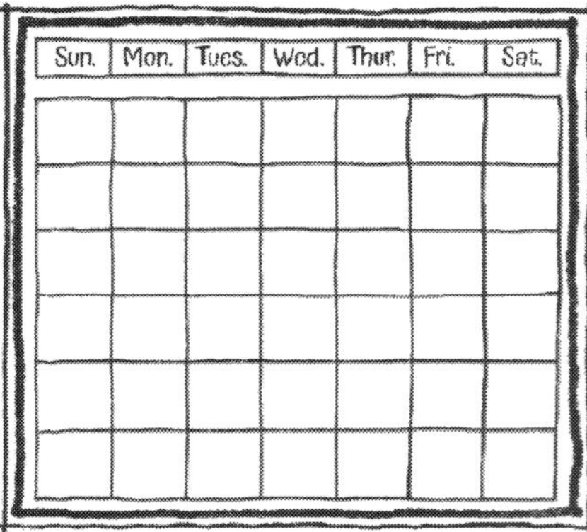

Month:

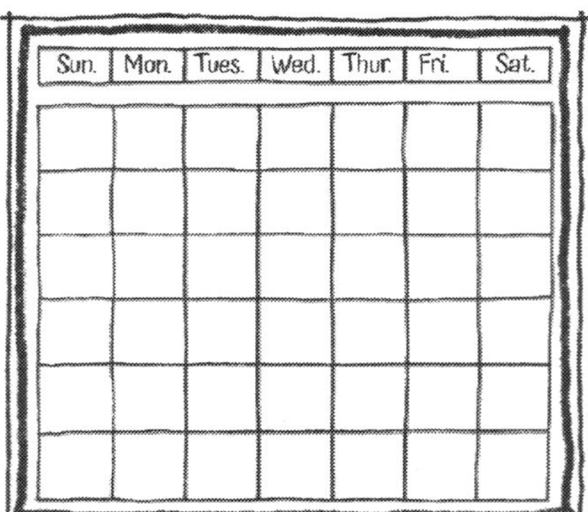

Month:

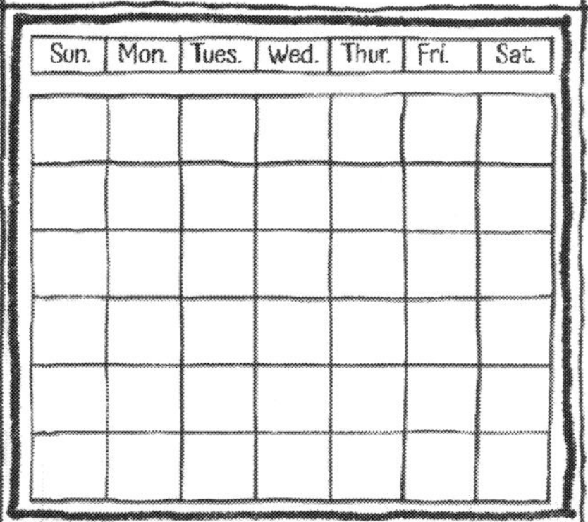

Month:

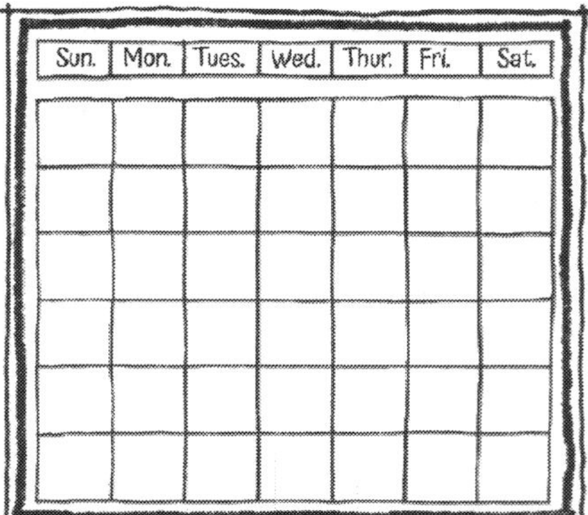

More Events & Opportunities

List important events and transfer them to your main planner.

- [ ]
- [ ]
- [ ]
- [ ]
- [ ]
- [ ]
- [ ]
- [ ]
- [ ]
- [ ]
- [ ]
- [ ]
- [ ]
- [ ]
- [ ]
- [ ]

ReSearch

Use this space to keep track of the research topics.

Topics:

Day/Time: Location: Speaker:

Title:

Day/Time: Location: Speaker:

Title:

Day/Time: Location: Speaker:

Title:

Day/Time: Location: Speaker:

Title:

Day/Time: Location: Speaker:

Title:

Day/Time: Location: Speaker:

Title:

Day/Time: Location: Speaker:

Title:

Skills, Ideas, & Topics

Take note of tools, software, or resources you will need.

- [ ]
- [ ]
- [ ]
- [ ]
- [ ]
- [ ]
- [ ]
- [ ]
- [ ]
- [ ]
- [ ]
- [ ]
- [ ]

GO-TO Section: Add your pages to TOC on page 29

ReSearch

Use this space to keep track of the research topics.

Topics:

Day/Time: Location: Speaker:

Title:

Day/Time: Location: Speaker:

Title:

Day/Time: Location: Speaker:

Title:

Day/Time: Location: Speaker:

Title:

Day/Time: Location: Speaker:

Title:

Day/Time: Location: Speaker:

Title:

Day/Time: Location: Speaker:

Title:

Skills, Ideas, & Topics

Take note of tools, software, or resources you will need.

- [ ]
- [ ]
- [ ]
- [ ]
- [ ]
- [ ]
- [ ]
- [ ]
- [ ]
- [ ]
- [ ]
- [ ]
- [ ]

GO-TO Section: Add your pages to TOC on page 29

Research

Use this space to keep track of the research topics.

Topics:

Day/Time: Location: Speaker:

Title:

Day/Time: Location: Speaker:

Title:

Day/Time: Location: Speaker:

Title:

Day/Time: Location: Speaker:

Title:

Day/Time: Location: Speaker:

Title:

Day/Time: Location: Speaker:

Title:

Day/Time: Location: Speaker:

Title:

Skills, Ideas, & Topics

Take note of tools, software, or resources you will need.

- [ ]
- [ ]
- [ ]
- [ ]
- [ ]
- [ ]
- [ ]
- [ ]
- [ ]
- [ ]
- [ ]
- [ ]
- [ ]

Research

Use this space to keep track of the research topics.

Topics:

Day/Time: Location: Speaker:
Title:

Day/Time: Location: Speaker:
Title:

Day/Time: Location: Speaker:
Title:

Day/Time: Location: Speaker:
Title:

Day/Time: Location: Speaker:
Title:

Day/Time: Location: Speaker:
Title:

Day/Time: Location: Speaker:
Title:

Skills, Ideas, & Topics

Take note of tools, software, or resources you will need.

- [ ]
- [ ]
- [ ]
- [ ]
- [ ]
- [ ]
- [ ]
- [ ]
- [ ]
- [ ]
- [ ]
- [ ]
- [ ]

GO-TO Section: Add your pages to TOC on page 29

ReSearch

Use this space to keep track of the research topics.

Topics:

Day/Time: Location: Speaker:

Title:

Day/Time: Location: Speaker:

Title:

Day/Time: Location: Speaker:

Title:

Day/Time: Location: Speaker:

Title:

Day/Time: Location: Speaker:

Title:

Day/Time: Location: Speaker:

Title:

Day/Time: Location: Speaker:

Title:

Skills, Ideas, & Topics

Take note of tools, software, or resources you will need.

- [ ]
- [ ]
- [ ]
- [ ]
- [ ]
- [ ]
- [ ]
- [ ]
- [ ]
- [ ]
- [ ]
- [ ]
- [ ]

GO-TO Section: Add your pages to TOC on page 29

Speaker & Teacher Information

List information about any of the speakers or their classes.

More Information

List more information and add details about their specialties.

☐

☐

☐

☐

☐

☐

☐

☐

☐

☐

☐

☐

☐

Appointments

List instructors or businesses you might want to connect with later.

Appointments

Day/Time: ______ Name: ______

Notes: ______

Day/Time: ______ Name: ______

Notes: ______

Day/Time: ______ Name: ______

Notes: ______

Day/Time: ______ Name: ______

Notes: ______

Day/Time: ______ Name: ______

Notes: ______

Day/Time: ______ Name: ______

Notes: ______

Day/Time: ______ Name: ______

Notes: ______

Day/Time: ______ Name: ______

Notes: ______

Collaborate & Communicate

Meetings & Coffee Chats

List all your other meetings and times to connect with others.
Or schedule time to chat with another student or new connection.

Appointments

Day/Time: Name:

Notes:

Day/Time: Name:

Notes:

Day/Time: Name:

Notes:

Day/Time: Name:

Notes:

Day/Time: Name:

Notes:

Day/Time: Name:

Notes:

Day/Time: Name:

Notes:

Day/Time: Name:

Notes:

Virtual Conference Class & Course Notes:

Notes Section Divider

Table of Contents

Use this table of contents page to keep course notes organized.

Notes

Date:
Time:
Location/URL:

Conference, class, or course notes

Title:
Speaker:

...and more notes !

Continue notes here & check out the "Go-To" section to help you organize.

GO-TO Section: Add your pages to TOC on page 29

Notes

Date:

Time:

Location/URL:

Conference, class, or course notes

Title:

Speaker:

...and more notes !

Continue notes here & check out the "Go-To" Section to help you organize.

Notes

Date:
Time:
Location/URL:

Conference, class, or course notes

Title:
Speaker:

...and more notes !

Continue notes here & check out the "Go-To" Section to help you organize.

GO-TO Section: Add your pages to TOC on page 29

Notes

Date:

Time:

Location/URL:

Conference, class, or course notes

Title:

Speaker:

...and more notes !

Continue notes here & check out the "Go-To" section to help you organize.

Notes

Date:

Time:

Location/URL:

Conference, class, or course notes

Title:

Speaker:

...and more notes !

Continue notes here & check out the "Go-To" section to help you organize.

GO-TO Section: Add your pages to TOC on page 29

Notes

Date:

Time:

Location/URL:

Conference, class, or course notes

Title:

Speaker:

...and more notes !

Continue notes here & check out the "Go-To" section to help you organize.

GO-TO Section: Add your pages to TOC on page 29

Notes

Date:

Time:

Location/URL:

Conference, class, or course notes

Title:

Speaker:

...and more notes !

Continue notes here & check out the "Go-To" section to help you organize.

Notes

Date:

Time:

Location/URL:

Conference, class, or course notes

Title:

Speaker:

...and more notes !

Continue notes here & check out the "Go-To" section to help you organize.

GO-TO Section: Add your pages to TOC on page 29

Notes

Date:
Time:
Location/URL:

Conference, class, or course notes

Title:

Speaker:

...and more notes !

Continue notes here & check out the "Go-To" Section to help you organize.

GO-TO Section: Add your pages to TOC on page 29

Notes

Date:

Time:

Location/URL:

Conference, class, or course notes

Title:

Speaker:

...and more notes !

Continue notes here & check out the "Go-To" section to help you organize.

GO-TO Section: Add your pages to TOC on page 29

Notes

Date:
Time:
Location/URL:

Conference, class, or course notes

Title:
Speaker:

...and more notes !

Continue notes here & check out the "Go-To" section to help you organize.

GO-TO Section: Add your pages to TOC on page 29

Notes

Date:
Time:
Location/URL:

Conference, class, or course notes

Title:
Speaker:

...and more notes !

Continue notes here & check out the "Go-To" section to help you organize.

GO-TO Section: Add your pages to TOC on page 29

Notes

Date:

Time:

Location/URL:

Conference, class, or course notes

Title:

Speaker:

...and more notes !

Continue notes here & check out the "Go-To" section to help you organize.

GO-TO Section: Add your pages to TOC on page 29

Notes

Date:

Time:

Location/URL:

Conference, class, or course notes

Title:

Speaker:

...and more notes !

Continue notes here & check out the "Go-To" section to help you organize.

GO-TO Section: Add your pages to TOC on page 29

Notes

Date:

Time:

Location/URL:

Conference, class, or course notes

Title:

Speaker:

...and more notes !

Continue notes here & check out the "Go-To" section to help you organize.

GO-TO Section: Add your pages to TOC on page 29

Notes

Date:

Time:

Location/URL:

Conference, class, or course notes

Title:

Speaker:

...and more notes !

Continue notes here & check out the "Go-To" section to help you organize.

GO-TO Section: Add your pages to TOC on page 29

Notes

Date:

Time:

Location/URL:

Conference, class, or course notes

Title:

Speaker:

...and more notes !

Continue notes here & check out the "Go-To" section to help you organize.

GO-TO Section: Add your pages to TOC on page 29

Notes

Date:

Time:

Location/URL:

Conference, class, or course notes

Title:

Speaker:

...and more notes !

Continue notes here & check out the "Go-To" section to help you organize.

GO-TO Section: Add your pages to TOC on page 29

Notes

Date:
Time:
Location/URL:

Conference, class, or course notes

Title:
Speaker:

...and more notes !

Continue notes here & check out the "Go-To" Section to help you organize.

Notes

Date:
Time:
Location/URL:

Conference, class, or course notes

Title:
Speaker:

...and more notes !

Continue notes here & check out the "Go-To" section to help you organize.

GO-TO Section: Add your pages to TOC on page 29

Notes

Date:
Time:
Location/URL:

Conference, class, or course notes

Title:
Speaker:

...and more notes !

Continue notes here & check out the "Go-To" section to help you organize.

GO-TO Section: Add your pages to TOC on page 29

Notes

Date:
Time:
Location/URL:

Conference, class, or course notes

Title:
Speaker:

...and more notes !

Continue notes here & check out the "Go-To" section to help you organize.

GO-TO Section: Add your pages to TOC on page 29

Notes

Date:

Time:

Location/URL:

Conference, class, or course notes

Title:

Speaker:

...and more notes !

Continue notes here & check out the "Go-To" section to help you organize.

GO-TO Section: Add your pages to TOC on page 29

Notes

Date:
Time:
Location/URL:

Conference, class, or course notes

Title:
Speaker:

...and more notes !

Continue notes here & check out the "Go-To" Section to help you organize.

GO-TO Section: Add your pages to TOC on page 29

Notes

Date:

Time:

Location/URL:

Conference, class, or course notes

Title:

Speaker:

...and more notes !

Continue notes here & check out the "Go-To" Section to help you organize.

Notes

Date:
Time:
Location/URL:

Conference, class, or course notes

Title:

Speaker:

...and more notes !

Continue notes here & check out the "Go-To" section to help you organize.

GO-TO Section: Add your pages to TOC on page 29

Notes

Date:
Time:
Location/URL:

Conference, class, or course notes

Title:
Speaker:

...and more notes !

Continue notes here & check out the "Go-To" section to help you organize.

Notes

Date:

Time:

Location/URL:

Conference, class, or course notes

Title:

Speaker:

...and more notes !

Continue notes here & check out the "Go-To" section to help you organize.

Notes

Date:

Time:

Location/URL:

Conference, class, or course notes

Title:

Speaker:

...and more notes !

Continue notes here & check out the "Go-To" section to help you organize.

GO-TO Section: Add your pages to TOC on page 29

Notes

Date:

Time:

Location/URL:

Conference, class, or course notes

Title:

Speaker:

...and more notes !

Continue notes here & check out the "Go-To" section to help you organize.

GO-TO Section: Add your pages to TOC on page 29

Notes

Date:

Time:

Location/URL:

Conference, class, or course notes

Title:

Speaker:

...and more notes !

Continue notes here & check out the "Go-To" section to help you organize.

GO-TO Section: Add your pages to TOC on page 29

Notes

Date:
Time:
Location/URL:

Conference, class, or course notes

Title:
Speaker:

...and more notes !

Continue notes here & check out the "Go-To" Section to help you organize.

Notes

Date:

Time:

Location/URL:

Conference, class, or course notes

Title:

Speaker:

...and more notes !

Continue notes here & check out the "Go-To" section to help you organize.

GO-TO Section: Add your pages to TOC on page 29

Notes

Date:

Time:

Location/URL:

Conference, class, or course notes

Title:

Speaker:

...and more notes !

Continue notes here & check out the "Go-To" Section to help you organize.

GO-TO Section: Add your pages to TOC on page 29

Notes

Date:

Time:

Location/URL:

Conference, class, or course notes

Title:

Speaker:

...and more notes !

Continue notes here & check out the "Go-To" Section to help you organize.

Notes

Date:

Time:

Location/URL:

Conference, class, or course notes

Title:

Speaker:

...and more notes !

Continue notes here & check out the "Go-To" Section to help you organize.

Notes

Date:
Time:
Location/URL:

Conference, class, or course notes

Title:
Speaker:

...and more notes !

Continue notes here & check out the "Go-To" section to help you organize.

GO-TO Section: Add your pages to TOC on page 29

Notes

Date:
Time:
Location/URL:

Conference, class, or course notes

Title:

Speaker:

...and more notes !

Continue notes here & check out the "Go-To" Section to help you organize.

GO-TO Section: Add your pages to TOC on page 29

Notes

Date:
Time:
Location/URL:

Conference, class, or course notes

Title:

Speaker:

...and more notes !

Continue notes here & check out the "Go-To" section to help you organize.

GO-TO Section: Add your pages to TOC on page 29

Notes

Date:
Time:
Location/URL:

Conference, class, or course notes

Title:

Speaker:

...and more notes !

Continue notes here & check out the "Go-To" section to help you organize.

GO-TO Section: Add your pages to TOC on page 29

Notes

Date:
Time:
Location/URL:

Conference, class, or course notes

Title:

Speaker:

...and more notes !

Continue notes here & check out the "Go-To" Section to help you organize.

GO-TO Section: Add your pages to TOC on page 29

Notes

Date:
Time:
Location/URL:

Conference, class, or course notes

Title:

Speaker:

...and more notes !

Continue notes here & check out the "Go-To" section to help you organize.

GO-TO Section: Add your pages to TOC on page 29

Notes

Date:
Time:
Location/URL:

Conference, class, or course notes

Title:

Speaker:

...and more notes !

Continue notes here & check out the "Go-To" Section to help you organize.

GO-TO Section: Add your pages to TOC on page 29

Notes

Date:
Time:
Location/URL:

Conference, class, or course notes

Title:
Speaker:

...and more notes !

Continue notes here & check out the "Go-To" Section to help you organize.

GO-TO Section: Add your pages to TOC on page 29

Coloring & Doodle Page

Fill in & color the patterns below

Practice Coloring Patterns

Draw & design your own patterns

Textures from Lines

Color the patterns and add extra lines.

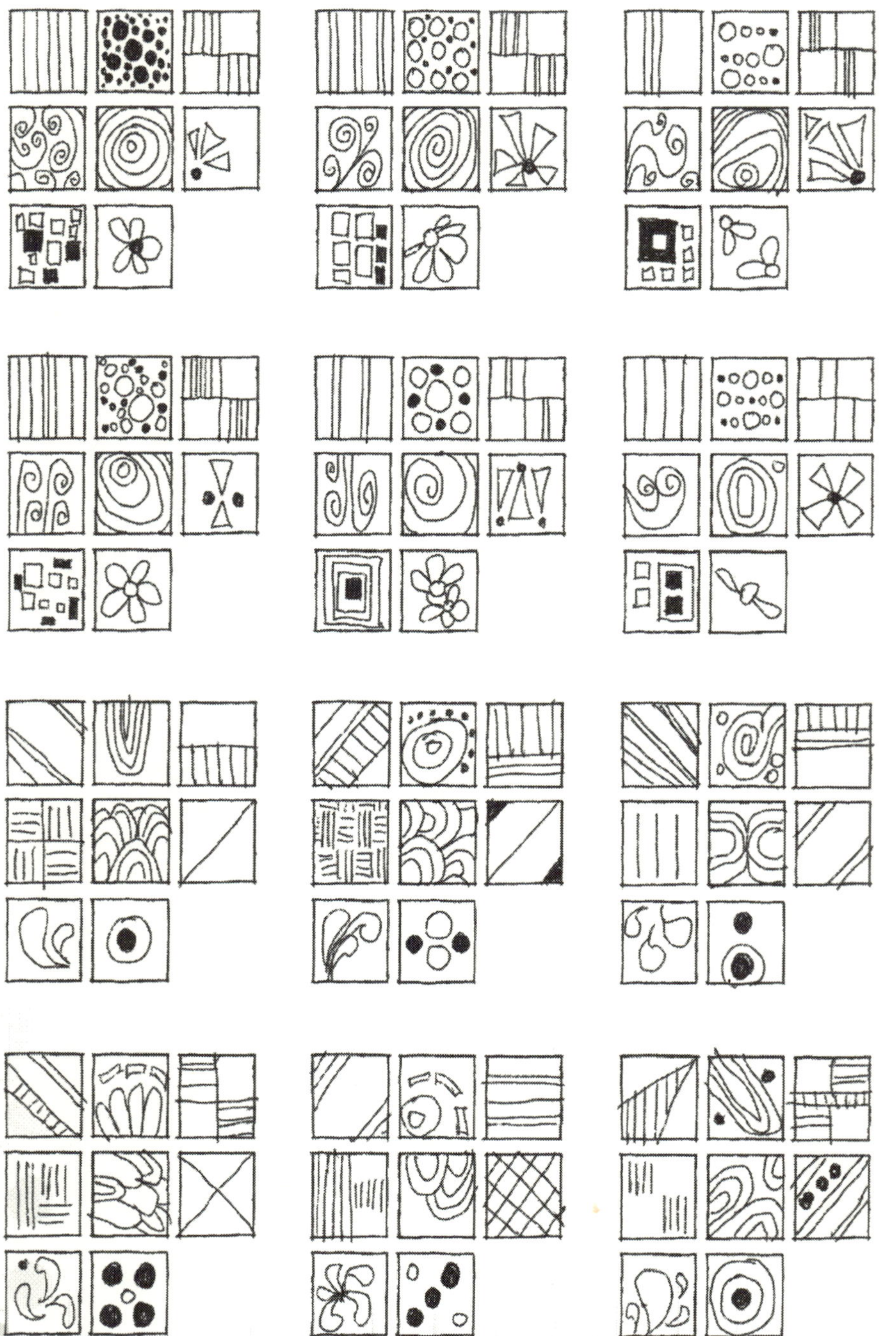

Practice Tracing the Lines

Trace over the gray patterns and color.

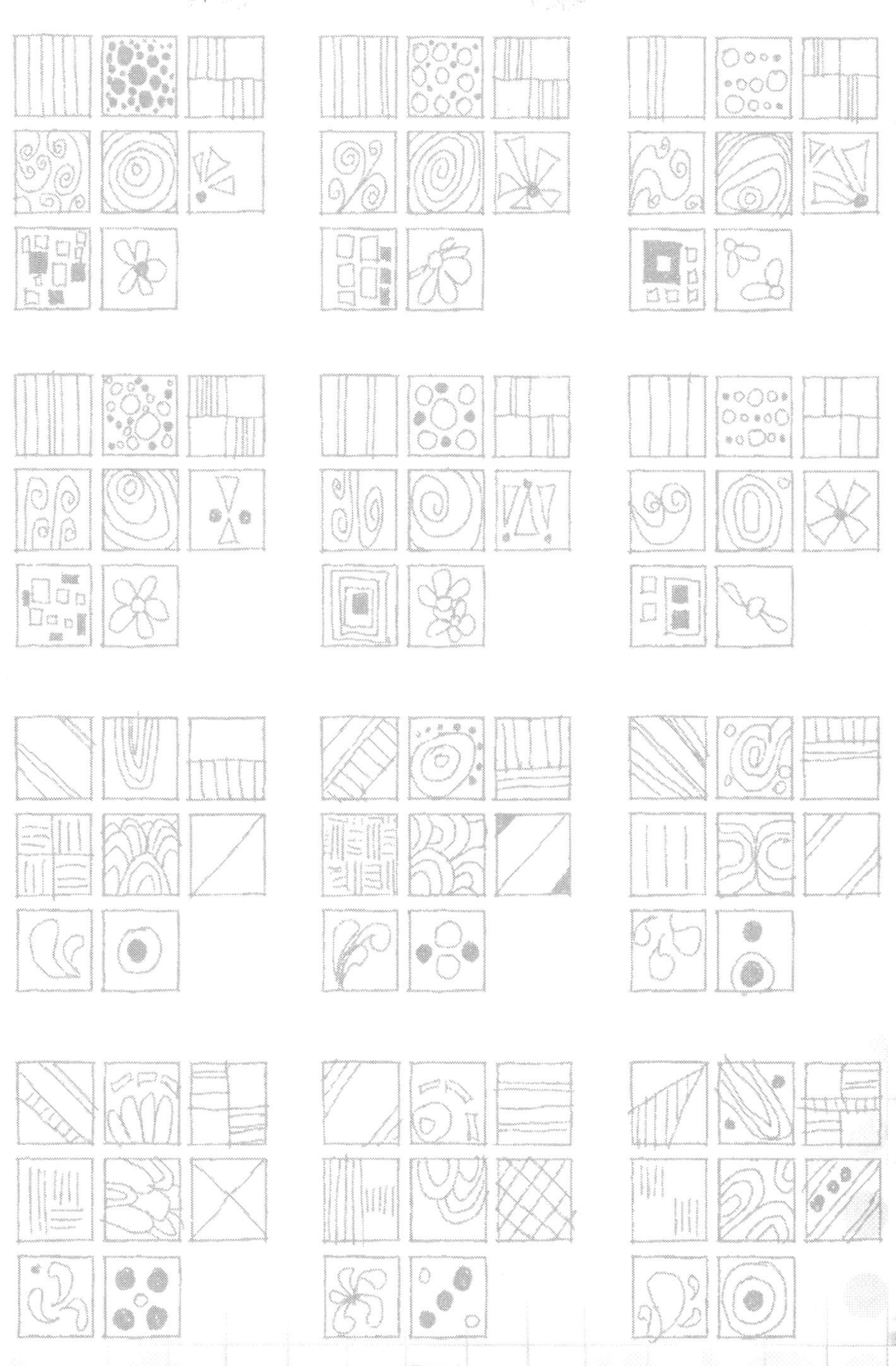

Lettering Doodles

Try this lettering style by drawing over the letters

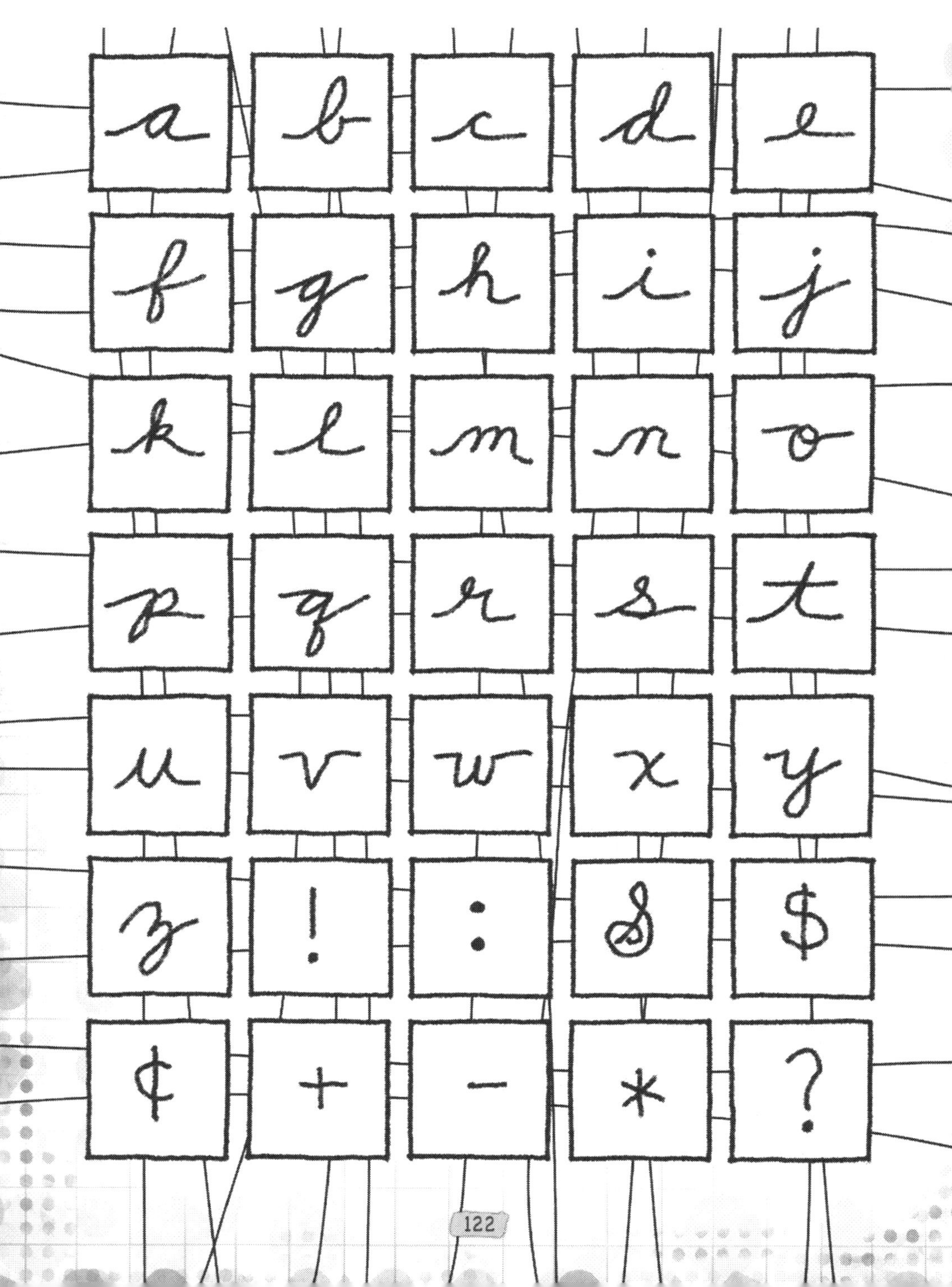

Practice Doodling Letters

Now try your own lettering or color the squares

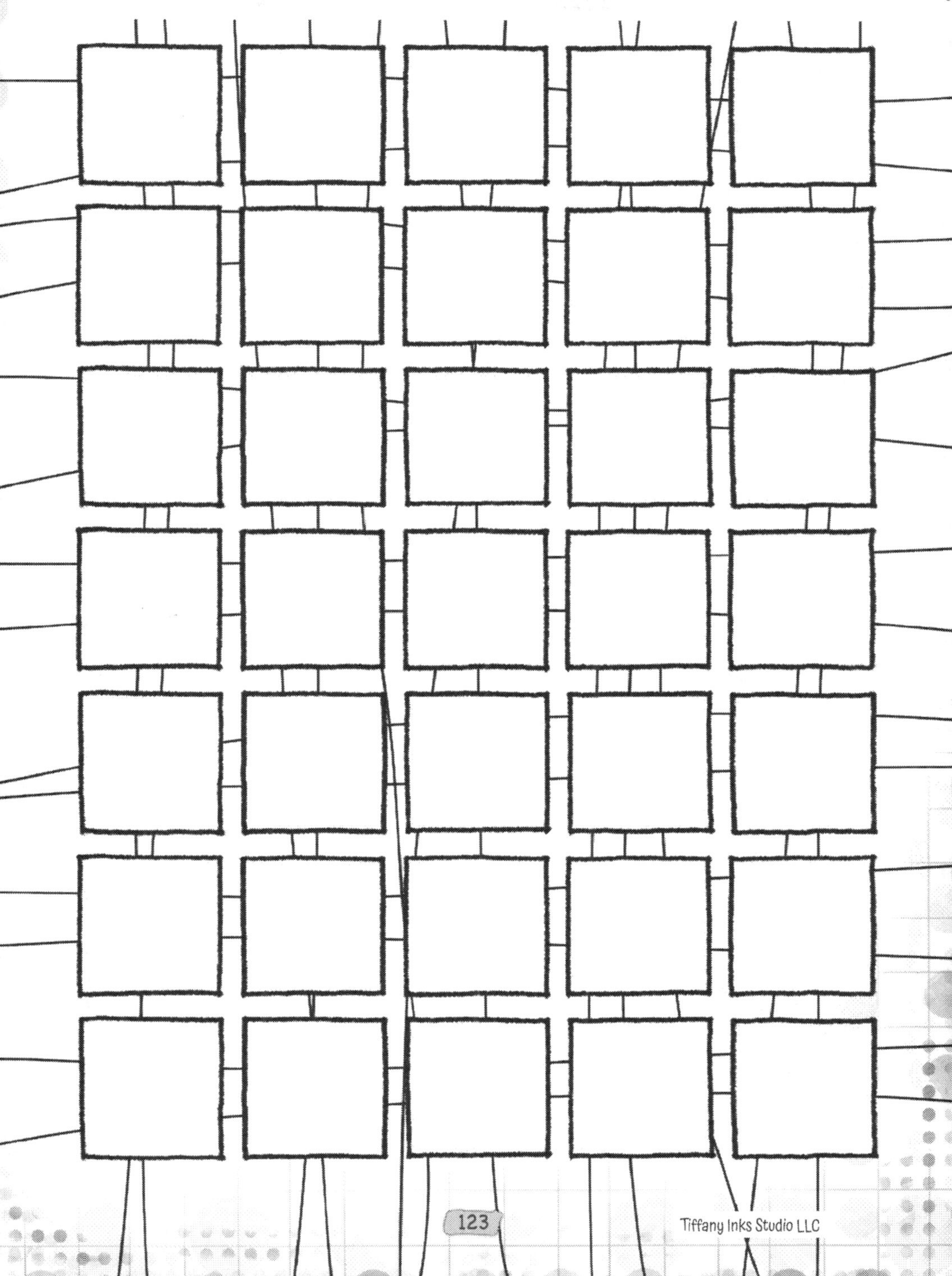

Sketching

Use this space for creative note-taking or sketching.

Drawing

Use this space to draw an idea or take notes on bullet pages.

Vision Board Doodling

Use this space for creating a vision for your brand, your project, your ministry, or your website. Be creative and dream.

word list

1
2
3
4
5
6
7

visision
creativity
goals

Goals & Objectives

List 3 goals for this journal. Write objectives to reach those goals and make plans to add these to your action plan.

goal #1

1
2
3
4
5
6
7

goal #2

1
2
3
4
5
6
7

goal #3

1
2
3
4
5
6
7

List of Books or References

If someone mentioned a book or a writing reference title, write it here. Do you own it? Do you have it on Kindle? Are you borrowing it? Want to buy it?

		Own Book	Kindle-ebook	Want to Buy	Borrowed	Other
☐	______________________	☐	☐	☐	☐	☐
☐	______________________	☐	☐	☐	☐	☐
☐	______________________	☐	☐	☐	☐	☐
☐	______________________	☐	☐	☐	☐	☐
☐	______________________	☐	☐	☐	☐	☐
☐	______________________	☐	☐	☐	☐	☐
☐	______________________	☐	☐	☐	☐	☐
☐	______________________	☐	☐	☐	☐	☐
☐	______________________	☐	☐	☐	☐	☐
☐	______________________	☐	☐	☐	☐	☐
☐	______________________	☐	☐	☐	☐	☐
☐	______________________	☐	☐	☐	☐	☐
☐	______________________	☐	☐	☐	☐	☐
☐	______________________	☐	☐	☐	☐	☐
☐	______________________	☐	☐	☐	☐	☐
☐	______________________	☐	☐	☐	☐	☐
☐	______________________	☐	☐	☐	☐	☐
☐	______________________	☐	☐	☐	☐	☐

List of Movies, TV, or Film

If someone mentioned a movie, film or TV title, write it here. Have you seen it? Do you own it? Are you borrowing it? Want to buy it?

	Title	Own Book	Kindle-ebook	Want to Buy	Borrowed	Other
☐	______	☐	☐	☐	☐	☐
☐	______	☐	☐	☐	☐	☐
☐	______	☐	☐	☐	☐	☐
☐	______	☐	☐	☐	☐	☐
☐	______	☐	☐	☐	☐	☐
☐	______	☐	☐	☐	☐	☐
☐	______	☐	☐	☐	☐	☐
☐	______	☐	☐	☐	☐	☐
☐	______	☐	☐	☐	☐	☐
☐	______	☐	☐	☐	☐	☐
☐	______	☐	☐	☐	☐	☐
☐	______	☐	☐	☐	☐	☐
☐	______	☐	☐	☐	☐	☐
☐	______	☐	☐	☐	☐	☐
☐	______	☐	☐	☐	☐	☐
☐	______	☐	☐	☐	☐	☐
☐	______	☐	☐	☐	☐	☐
☐	______	☐	☐	☐	☐	☐

Quotes to Remember

Create an artsy page of quotes to remember.

Scripture Verse References

Letter a Bible verse which illustrates a theme for your project.

Plot Inspirations & Threads

Jot down your ideas for plot threads.

- [ ]
- [ ]
- [ ]
- [ ]
- [ ]
- [ ]
- [ ]
- [ ]
- [ ]
- [ ]
- [ ]
- [ ]
- [ ]
- [ ]
- [ ]
- [ ]

Character Sketches & Ideas

Jot down your ideas for new or existing characters.

Name: ☐

Name ☐

Name ☐

Name ☐

Name ☐

Name ☐

Name ☐

Name ☐

Name ☐

Name ☐

Places, Settings, & World Design

Jot down your ideas for place setting or worlds.

Place: ☐

Place: ☐

Place: ☐

Place: ☐

Social Media Ideas

How can you sharing your ministry, ideas, products, and your heart?

- [ ] ____________________
- [ ] ____________________
- [ ] ____________________
- [ ] ____________________
- [ ] ____________________
- [ ] ____________________
- [ ] ____________________
- [ ] ____________________
- [ ] ____________________

Social Media Planning Days

Use this space to record which days you plan to do each social media platform. Make note of times by using a color coded key.

KEY: ☐ ☐ ☐ ☐ ☐ ☐ ☐ ☐ ☐

	Sharing on each Platform:	Su	M	T	W	T	F	Sa
☐	______________________	☐	☐	☐	☐	☐	☐	☐
☐	______________________	☐	☐	☐	☐	☐	☐	☐
☐	______________________	☐	☐	☐	☐	☐	☐	☐
☐	______________________	☐	☐	☐	☐	☐	☐	☐
☐	______________________	☐	☐	☐	☐	☐	☐	☐
☐	______________________	☐	☐	☐	☐	☐	☐	☐
☐	______________________	☐	☐	☐	☐	☐	☐	☐
☐	______________________	☐	☐	☐	☐	☐	☐	☐
☐	______________________	☐	☐	☐	☐	☐	☐	☐
☐	______________________	☐	☐	☐	☐	☐	☐	☐
☐	______________________	☐	☐	☐	☐	☐	☐	☐
☐	______________________	☐	☐	☐	☐	☐	☐	☐
☐	______________________	☐	☐	☐	☐	☐	☐	☐
☐	______________________	☐	☐	☐	☐	☐	☐	☐
☐	______________________	☐	☐	☐	☐	☐	☐	☐
☐	______________________	☐	☐	☐	☐	☐	☐	☐
☐	______________________	☐	☐	☐	☐	☐	☐	☐
☐	______________________	☐	☐	☐	☐	☐	☐	☐

Praise

List what you are grateful for and let thankfulness flow.

- [ ]
- [ ]
- [ ]
- [ ]
- [ ]
- [ ]
- [ ]
- [ ]
- [ ]
- [ ]
- [ ]
- [ ]
- [ ]
- [ ]
- [ ]
- [ ]

gratitude

Prayers

Write prayers for yourself and others.

- [ ]
- [ ]
- [ ]
- [ ]
- [ ]
- [ ]
- [ ]
- [ ]
- [ ]
- [ ]
- [ ]
- [ ]
- [ ]
- [ ]
- [ ]

requests

Praise

List what you are grateful for and let thankfulness flow.

☐

☐

☐

☐

☐

☐

☐

☐

☐

☐

☐

☐

☐

☐

☐

☐

gratitude

Prayers

Write prayers for yourself and others.

- [ ]
- [ ]
- [ ]
- [ ]
- [ ]
- [ ]
- [ ]
- [ ]
- [ ]
- [ ]
- [ ]
- [ ]
- [ ]
- [ ]
- [ ]
- [ ]

requests

Application Notes

Add application topics of possible future action or goals.

- [ ]
- [ ]
- [ ]
- [ ]
- [ ]
- [ ]
- [ ]
- [ ]
- [ ]
- [ ]
- [ ]
- [ ]
- [ ]
- [ ]
- [ ]
- [ ]

3 Main Take-Aways

List the top 3 take-aways from your studies. Add them to the "Action Plan."

application time

1

- [ ]
- [ ]
- [ ]

2

- [ ]
- [ ]
- [ ]

3

- [ ]
- [ ]
- [ ]

Action Plan Questions

Fill in the name of the month & days. Refer to this page for goals & events.

- [ ]
- [ ]
- [ ]
- [ ]
- [ ]
- [ ]
- [ ]
- [ ]
- [ ]
- [ ]
- [ ]
- [ ]
- [ ]
- [ ]
- [ ]
- [ ]

Action Plan Milestones

Use this space to record your next steps and actionable goal setting markers.

- [ ]
- [ ]
- [ ]
- [ ]
- [ ]
- [ ]
- [ ]
- [ ]
- [ ]
- [ ]
- [ ]
- [ ]
- [ ]
- [ ]
- [ ]
- [ ]

Oh, the People I've Met!

List those you would like to stay in touch with and send thank you notes.

Patricia Tiffany Morris

Owner of Tiffany Inks Studio LLC

WEBSITE: https://www.patriciatiffanymorris.com

PINTEREST: https://www.pinterest.com/patriciatiffanymorris/

FACEBOOK: https://www.facebook.com/PatriciaTiffanyMorris

TIKTOK: https://www.tiktok.com/@journalingscribbles

TWITTER: https://twitter.com/PatTiffanyInks

IG WRITER: https://www.instagram.com/PatriciaTiffanyMorrisWriter/

FB WRITER PAGE: https://www.facebook.com/PatTiffanyInks

LINKEDIN: https://www.linkedin.com/in/patricia-tiffany-morris

ETSY SHOP: https://www.etsy.com/shop/TiffanyInksStudio

YOUTUBE: https://www.youtube.com/c/PatriciaTiffanyMorris

AMAZON: https://www.amazon.com/author/patriciatiffanymorris

GOODREADS: https://www.goodreads.com/author/show/19529431.Patricia_Tiffany_Morris

Author Biography

An incorrigible writer, passionate artist, and eclectic creative, **Patricia Tiffany Morris** sketches ideas in her sleep, that is when she takes time to sleep. All night reading and studying served her well during architectural design studio at ISU in the eighties where she soaked up engineering and computer skills.

Now an empty-nester, she's inspired by her rhyming husband, who reads her suspense-filled fiction in delightful character voices and helps her brainstorm plot threads. She adores Pinterest and hashtags, but finds Twitter quirky.

Patricia actively supports fellow authors and offers geeky tech services for a minimal price & adores teaching others.

Her goal to share Christ through inspirational fictional stories brought her numerous awards from 2019-2021 in poetry, short fiction, children's stories, and suspense & women's fiction, including 1st place at BRMCWC for her upcoming split-time novel. Her publishing credits include The Ekphrastic Review, Word Weavers International, Guideposts, and other publications. Visit her blog for inspiration and find her on social media.

Faith-inspired artist

A Collection of Journals, Notebooks, Logbooks, and Planners for Creativity & Organization

Which one will you choose next?

Each book fits into one of 9 different color-coded categories.
Some journals have a variety of cover options.

Future editions or versions will be marked on the front cover.

Categories:

1 planners
2 Writing
3 Spiritual Life
4 Family & friends
5 HOUSE & THINGS
6 adventures
7 Creativity
8 Projects & Activities
9 wellness

creativity & organization

www.patriciatiffanymorris.com

In a variety of covers & editions

Published by Tiffany Inks Studio LLC

Tiffany Inks Studio LLC

Offering a variety of covers & editions

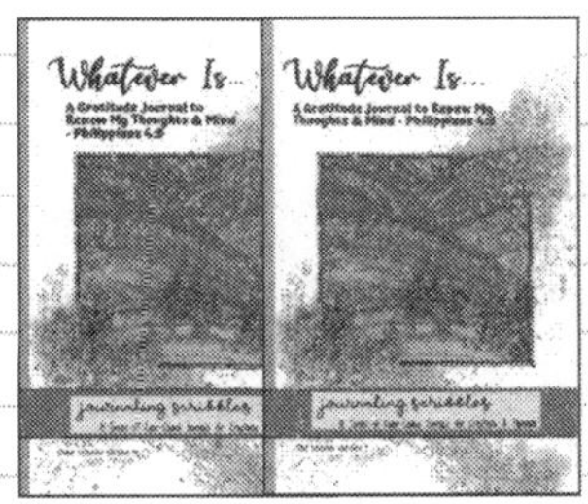

Journaling Scribbles™ Collection

creativity **journals** for writers

If you have a special journaling project in mind,

contact Tiffany Inks Studio LLC for more information.

What are your next Steps?

- **Add appointments to your calendar.**
- **Refine your goals and objectives.**
- **Send thank you notes.**
- **Update your references or contacts.**
- **Work on your social media plan.**
- **Keep in touch with new connections.**

What Skill will you learn next?

please know that i am praying for you.

If you have a journal page to share, tag us on social media.

IG @PatriciaTiffanyMorris or on FB @TiffanyInksStudio

Made in the USA
Middletown, DE
09 November 2021